A Week in the North

by Carmel Reilly

OXFORD
UNIVERSITY PRESS
AUSTRALIA & NEW ZEALAND

We had a week in the north.
It was good fun.

This was my room.

I am at the market. We shop for food.

Dad is at the market, too.

Look at Mum. She is going for a surf.

Mum is good at surfing.

Dad took me to the port.

We see boats sailing.

At night we had rain.

Mum took shots of the light.

A lot of rain fell on the road.

You can see my things got wet, too.

We took the dog for a run.

We ran to the park and back.

I had fun in the north.